For the Hope
of Humanity

For the Hope of Humanity

The Doctrine of the Dormition of the Theotokos in Orthodox Christian Tradition

Michael George Tsichlis, PhD

St. Irenaeus Orthodox Theological Institute
St. Louis, Missouri, USA

iUniverse, Inc.
Bloomington

For the Hope of Humanity
The Doctrine of the Dormition of the Theotokos
in Orthodox Christian Tradition

iUniverse books may be ordered through booksellers or by contacting:

iUniverse
1663 Liberty Drive
Bloomington, IN 47403
www.iuniverse.com
1-800-Authors (1-800-288-4677)

Because of the dynamic nature of the Internet, any web addresses or links contained in this book may have changed since publication and may no longer be valid.

Any people depicted in stock imagery provided by Thinkstock are models, and such images are being used for illustrative purposes only.
Certain stock imagery © Thinkstock.

ISBN: 978-1-4620-3487-1 (sc)
ISBN: 978-1-4620-3488-8 (ebk)

Library of Congress Control Number: 2011911154

Printed in the United States of America

Cover Art: The Dormition of the Theotokos. *Icon painting on the ceiling of Assumption Greek Orthodox Church, St. Louis, Missouri. By the hands of iconographers Dimitrios Tsiantas and Nicholas Vlachogiannis. Reproduced with permission.*

iUniverse rev. date: 08/12/2011

To my late mother,
Thelma May Tsichlis.
May her memory be eternal!

"... [T]o ignore the Mother means to misinterpret the Son."

Rev. Georges Florovsky,
From "The Ever-Virgin Mother of God" in *Creation and Redemption, Volume 3 in the Collected Works of Georges Florovsky*

CONTENTS

ACKNOWLEDGEMENTS

There are several people I wish to thank for their help in making this small book a reality. First, I owe a special debt of gratitude to Sr. Patricia Walter, O.P., professor of systematic theology at Aquinas Institute of Theology in St. Louis, Missouri. Sr. Pat strongly encouraged me take on this little known subject as a research project, and offered much constructive advice along the way.

I also wish to thank the Very Rev. Dr. Steven Salaris of All Saints of North America Antiochian Orthodox Church and Rev. Michael Arbanas of St. Nicholas Greek Orthodox Church for their helpful review of the manuscript. Also, my heartfelt thanks go out to the Very Rev. Thomas Hopko, Dean Emeritus of St. Vladimir's Seminary, who offered invaluable reflection and input.

My special thanks as well to Mr. Chris Paradowski of St. Nicholas Greek Orthodox Church, who helped gather together most of the images that appear in this book, as well to Frs. Douglas Papulis, Joseph Strzelecki, and Steven Tsichlis for their assistance. Also, I wish to express my great appreciation to Rev. Archimandrite Ephrem Lash, whose beautiful, lucid translation of the Dormition services are appended to this book.

Finally, I'd be remiss not to thank the unending support of my wife, Vasilika Terss Tsichlis, for this project and many others, as well as the daily inspiration I receive from our son, George.

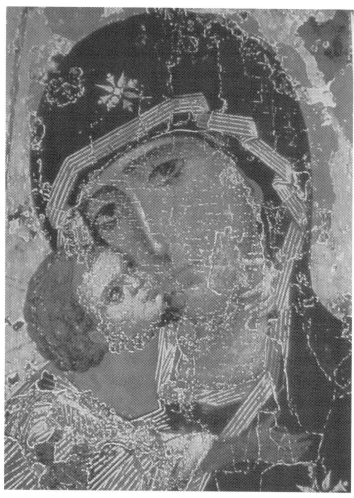

Icon: *The Virgin of Vladimir*, c. 1131. One of the best known iconographic images of the Mary and the Christ Child, it was painted in Constantinople and taken to Russia. It is a fine example of the *Eleousa* (tenderness, compassionate) form of Marian iconography

The Popular Yet Mysterious
Mother of Jesus

Even in the secular and "post-Christian" age of the early twenty-first century, Mary of Nazareth still claims a place in our cultural consciousness. While their knowledge of her may be limited, most people have at least heard of the mother of Jesus, if nothing else through her central role in the Nativity story. Even non-Christians living in the United States and other Western societies have probably been exposed at some time to an image or reference to Mary. Stories of miraculous visions, visitations, and intercessions by the Holy Virgin have emerged over the centuries down to modern times, as have phenomena such as weeping icons, which shed flowing tears from the painted eyes of Our Glorious Lady. Even non-Christians, such as Muslims, have long incorporated Mary into their own religious traditions, albeit through a very different narrative lens than the one commonly understood by Christians. Mary, although often incompletely and imperfectly known, remains a recognizable figure to people across the planet.

Yet for many, including Orthodox Christians, much about Mary is shrouded in mystery, appearing as a patchwork of idealized caricatures personifying quintessential womanhood, maternity, chastity, love, tenderness, compassion, and mercy. For most "cradle" Orthodox who grew up regularly attending worship services and Sunday school, Mary is more than anything understood as

Jesus' mother, the birth-giver of God, or *Theotokos*. This well-known image is continuously reinforced by ubiquitous icons featuring her graceful half-figure, gazing peacefully outward as she cradles her Son, to whom she may gesture with approval (a style of icon called the *Hodighitria*, or "She who points the way")—or tenderly caressing cheek to cheek with motherly affection (a style referred to as *Eleousa*, or "Our Lady of Tenderness").[1] In these images she appears to call out, inviting us with a simple hand gesture or nod to be attentive to her Son, the Incarnate Word of God. In all likelihood, such icons of the Theotokos were displayed in Orthodox Christians' homes—most often in their bedrooms—since the time of childhood. In addition, devotional practices such as kissing icons of Mary or making the sign of the cross at the mention of her name during the Divine Liturgy or other sacred services add a physical dimension to our acts of reverence.

---

[1]   Leonid Ouspensky, *The Theology of the Icon*, (Crestwood: St. Vladimir's Seminary Press, 1978), 72.

The Virgin *Hodighitria*, or "She who points the way."

In addition to venerating her as the Mother of God, Orthodox Christians proclaim Mary as the *Panagia*, or "All Holy", whose holiness, spotless purity, and perpetual virginity is celebrated in sacred hymns and proclaimed by fathers of the Church. The term also helps to designate her, as Metropolitan Kallistos Ware has written, as "the supreme example of synergy or cooperation between the deity and the free will of man."[2] It reveals much about her importance that there are multiple baptismal names for "Mary" in the Orthodox tradition. In addition to the Hebrew form of the name Miriam, from which the Greek and Latin derivatives are Maria or Mary in English, further derivatives include Marika, Marietta, Marian, and Marion, there is also Panagiota (female) and Panagiotis or Panos (male)—a literal reference to the All Holy Mother of God.[3]

Adult converts to the Orthodox faith may perceive Mary in a variety of ways, depending on their social and cultural backgrounds as well as their prior worship experiences, if any, that they bring to their acceptance of Orthodoxy. If they were fully catechized in the history, doctrine, and private and communal worship of the Church, they have been surely taught that she is, as we proclaim at each liturgy, "our most holy, pure, blessed, and glorious Lady the Mother of God and ever-virgin Mary,"[4] whom we commemorate

---

[2]   Timothy (Kallistos) Ware, *The Orthodox Church*, (London: Penguin Books, 1987), 263.

[3]   A comprehensive list of Greek Orthodox baptismal names can be found at *www.namedays.gr*.

[4]   The Nicene Creed and all quotes from the Divine Liturgy of St. John Chrysostom are excerpted from *The Divine Liturgy of St. John Chrysostom,* Faculty of Hellenic Holy

through the celebration of four major feast days designated in her honor on the church calendar, as well as a number of "lesser" feasts.* Also, as new and cradle Orthodox have been taught, we reach out to Mary in prayer, beseeching her to intercede on behalf of ourselves, our loved ones, and the entire world. Despite this, converts coming to Orthodoxy from other faith traditions may understandably continue to struggle for a time with Mary's large presence in church worship.

But the question lingers for Orthodox and non-Orthodox alike: who was this Nazarene woman, and why should we spend so much time in devotion to her? Mary, of course, is not to be confused with her Son, whom we acknowledge in the Nicene Creed as "the only Begotten Son of God" and the Savior of humanity. So why should she be held in such high regard and why, especially, should we accept as true a church doctrine that affirms that when her earthly life came to an end that she was taken, body and soul, into the presence of her Son in the Kingdom? After all, in our reading of the New Testament we find

---

Cross Greek Orthodox School of Theology, trans. (Brookline: Holy Cross Orthodox Press, 1985) 18-19.

' The major feasts of the Theotokos in the Orthodox Church are the Nativity of the Virgin (September 8); the Presentation of the Theotokos in the Temple (November 21); the Annunciation (March 25); and the Dormition (August 15). Several minor feasts include the Life-Giving Fount of the Theotokos (the Friday following Pascha); the Protection of the Theotokos (October 28 in the Greek tradition, October 1 in the Slavic); the Conception of the Theotokos by Righteous Anna (December 9); and the Synaxis of the Theotokos (December 26).

that only Jesus was raised in body and ascended into heaven. Indeed, we find only scattered information about the life of Mary in the Bible, and nothing is mentioned about her death!

Seeking Mary:

Sacred Tradition and Scripture

As Orthodox Christians, we acknowledge Holy Tradition as the source of God's revelation of truth delivered to his people through the words of the prophets and apostles and under the guidance of the Holy Spirit. For the Orthodox, the word "tradition" (from the Latin *tradere*) is understood in its scriptural context of "deliverance" or a "handing over" (in Greek *paradosis*) of the collective truths of the faith from the time of Christ and the Apostles through successive generations of the faithful.[5] Just as St. Paul exhorted the Thessalonians to "stand fast and hold to the traditions (*paradosis*) you were taught . . ." (2 Thess. 2:15) so too is it the responsibility of every Orthodox Christian to keep the integrity of his or her faith in the fullness of its beliefs and practices, so that it may be delivered whole to our progeny.[6]

As Orthodox, our understanding of Mary has also been "delivered" by the Holy Spirit through the collective Tradition of the Church. Indeed, what we do know of Mary's life and how we approach her in prayer and worship

---

[5]   Nicon D. Patrinacos, *A Dictionary of Greek Orthodoxy*. (Pleasantville: Hellenic Heritage Publications, 1987) 356-357.

[6]   John Meyendorff, *Living Tradition*. (Crestwood: St. Vladimir's Seminary Press, 1978) 21.

has been delivered to us not from merely one or even a few sources, but from many sources that make up the foundations of Marian dogmatic tradition: canonical and apocryphal scriptures; the writings of the Church Fathers; canons (ecclesiastical rules or laws); dogmatic pronouncements of universally accepted synods of bishops and the great ecumenical councils of the Church; as well as the development of our devotional and liturgical practices of worship, including hymnography and the use of sacred art and iconography, all of which date back to the early centuries of the Church.[7]

The primary foundational source within the Spirit-inspired Tradition of the Church, however, is Sacred Scripture, what has been described in one Orthodox catechism as "the main written source and inspiration of all that developed in later ages."[8] That the Bible holds central importance in the life of the Orthodox Church can be considered an understatement. The pervasive ecclesiastical use and veneration of scripture in liturgical services undeniably serves to prove that Orthodox worship is largely Bible-based. In addition to Gospel and Epistle readings, the Book of Gospels itself is kissed and held high in procession during various junctures in the liturgy. "Look carefully into the Scriptures, which are the true utterances of the Holy Spirit. Observe that nothing of an unjust or counterfeit character is written in them" wrote St. Clement

---

[7] Holy Apostles Convent. *The Life of the Virgin Mary, the Theotokos*. (Buena Vista, CO: Holy Apostles Convent, 1989) ii-xii.

[8] Thomas Hopko, *The Orthodox Faith*, Vol. 1 *Doctrine*, 2nd ed. (Orthodox Church in America, Department of Religious Education, 1976) 12.

of Rome to Christians in Corinth about 96 C.E.[9] "The Bible is the Book of the Church," points out contemporary Orthodox theologian Fr. Thomas Hopko. "Everything in the Church is judged by the Bible . . . . The Bible lives in the Church. It is an essential element of the organic wholeness of the Church."[10]

So where does Mary stand in light of the written Word of God? Although the Bible tells us very little about Mary's life, what it does say is absolutely essential to understanding her crucial role in the salvation of humanity. In the Gospel of Luke, where more verses appear in reference to Mary than in any other canonical book of scripture, the story of the Annunciation, (also told in a shorter version in Matthew emphasizing Joseph's role), both defines and secures her place in salvation history and launches what would become a growing tradition of Marian veneration. Verses 1:26-38 of the Lukan narrative tell of Mary's encounter with the Archangel Gabriel, a messenger from God who visits her to inform her that she will conceive a son "who will be called the Son of God." (Luke 1:35, NKJV). After some initial hesitation, the young Nazarene woman, who was likely no more than sixteen years old, replied in the affirmative, "let it be to me according to your word," (1:38) and the destiny of humanity was changed forever.

---

9   "1 Clement", in Phillip Schaff and Alexander Roberts, eds., *The Ante-Nicene Fathers*, Vol.1, (Peabody, MA: Hendrickson, 1999) 17.

10   Thomas Hopko, *All the Fullness of God*. (Crestwood: St. Vladimir's Seminary Press, 1982) 49-50.

St. Luke the Evangelist. Greek icon, fourteenth century,
Mount Athos.

The Annunciation

As the first human being to receive Jesus into her life and heart, Mary may also be understood to be the "first Christian." Her decision to freely and unconditionally accept the will of the Lord has been regarded as the *quintessential model* of the reception of God's grace and obedience to his will. With her consent God became Incarnate—the Divine Word was made flesh. She herself was aware of her unique role, and proclaimed so in a song of praise and thanksgiving she sang to her confidant and cousin, Elizabeth, that we call the *Magnificat* (from the Latin meaning "magnifies or praises"):

> And Mary said:
> My soul magnifies the Lord.
> And my spirit has rejoiced in God my Savior.
> For He has regarded the lowly state of His maidservant;
> For behold, henceforth all generations will call me blessed.
> For He who is mighty has done great things for me.
> And holy is His name. (Luke 1:46-49, NKJV)

The song is both jubilant and prophetic, as Mary's entire being not only rejoices "in God my Savior," but also prophesizes that reverence for her will be *perpetual.* (". . . henceforth all generations will call me blessed."). These verses, found in a gospel narrative written about fifty years after Christ's crucifixion and resurrection, are the earliest written testimonies of her unique standing within the larger story of the Christian salvation. It is here where Marian devotion begins.

Other references to Mary are scattered throughout the New Testament. Taken together, they form a coherent, if seemingly incomplete, narrative timeline. In the Gospel of Matthew, Joseph is reassured in a dream that his betrothed wife has not caused scandal by her appearance as a pregnant woman, but is actually fulfilling the Old Testament prophecy found in the Book of Isaiah that "'the virgin shall be with child, and bear a Son, and they shall call His name Immanuel,' which is translated, 'God with us.'" (Matthew 1:23, NKJV). This visionary statement not only provided Joseph the courage to stand beside Mary as her husband, but to also accept Jesus as his adoptive son. Joseph's vision also functions to further validate the virginal purity of Mary.

The Marian biblical narrative continues with the story of the Nativity of Jesus found in both Luke (2:1-20) and Matthew (1:18-25); the presentation of the child Jesus in the temple for the first time in accordance with Jewish law (Luke 2:22-23), and the flight of the Holy Family into Egypt (Matthew 2:13-15); the expression of her motherly anxiety as she finds the twelve-year-old Jesus who had been missing three days in the Temple in Jerusalem "sitting in the midst of the teachers, both listening to them and asking them questions" and who were "astonished at His understanding and answers." (Luke 2:46, NKJV).

As Jesus grows, Joseph departs the gospel narratives and Mary fades into the background as Jesus begins his ministry. She appears at the Wedding at Cana with Jesus and his disciples, and at her behest Jesus performs his first miracle—turning water to wine (John 2:1-11). She is also pointed out and contrasted along with other members of Jesus' family in Jerusalem (Mark 3:31-35, Matthew 12:46-50, Luke 8:19-21). 11. This encounter is particularly revealing, as Jesus himself identifies his Mother as an example of one who hears the word of God and acts upon it.[11]

[11]   Chris Maunder, "Mary in the New Testament and the Apocrypha." pp. 12-13 in *Mary, The Complete Resource*. Sarah

Η ΓΕΝΝΗCΙC   ΤΥ ΧΡΙCΤΥ.

The Nativity of Christ.

Jane Boss, ed. (Oxford: Oxford University Press, 2007).

The Presentation of Jesus in the temple and
the blessing of Simeon.

The Flight to Egypt by Joseph and Mary with the infant Jesus.
Stained glass rendition, St. Nicholas Greek Orthodox Church, St.
Louis, Missouri, USA.

Finally, according to the Gospel of John, she is there at the end of Jesus' earthly life just as she was at the beginning. Along with Mary Magdalene, Mary the spouse of Clopas, and the Apostle John, the Mother of God is present at her Incarnate Son's crucifixion. Among his final words, Christ calls out from the Cross, "Woman, behold your son!"(John 19:26). As noted in Orthodox biblical commentary, when Jesus addressed Mary as "woman" he is in fact using a unique scriptural title imparting respect, affection, dignity, and distinction.[12] Christ then calls to John, "Behold your mother!"(v. 27) and from that hour, the scripture tells us, John took Mary into his own home. Tradition has interpreted this to mean that "the Lord symbolically establishes Mary's role as the mother of all faithful disciples in every generation." It also further establishes her ever-virginity, for John would not have taken her into his home if she had other natural children who could have cared for her.[13]

Outside of the gospel narratives, New Testament references to Mary are few. The Book of Acts, attributed to Luke, briefly makes reference to her praying with the apostles soon after Jesus' Ascension into Heaven (1:14). Paul refers to her, but not by name, when writing in his letter to the Galatians of Christ being "born of a woman." (4:4). The vision of a woman giving birth to "a male child who will rule all nations" in Revelation 12:1-6 is thought by some to be an allegory to Mary giving birth to Christ. But

---

[12]   Commentary note for Jn. 19:25-27 in "The Book of John" in *The Orthodox Study Bible*. (Managing ed. J. Richard Ballew. Nashville: Thomas Nelson, 2008) [1463, NT].

[13]   Ibid.

the many missing details of the life of Mary are not left to ponder indefinitely. In the decades that followed the death of the last apostle, St. John the Theologian, sometime near the end of the first century, various works began to appear that sought to fill in the gospel narratives. These stories are ultimately valued not so much for their historical veracity as they are for what they reveal about the person and purpose of the Mother of God, and how the major watershed events of her life – including her death – teach us about true Christian faithfulness and discipleship.

The Descent of Christ from the Cross, late sixteenth century
icon from Crete.

The Ascension of Christ, with Mary
and the apostles present.

Early Extra-Biblical Narratives
of the Life of the Virgin Mary

By about 150 C.E. a written account of Mary's early life before the birth of Jesus emerged. Originally titled *The Nativity of Mary* and later *The Infancy Gospel of James*, it came to be commonly known as the *Protoevangelium of James*, referring to stories before (proto) the time of the gospels (evangelium).[14] Unlike the Christocentric New Testament gospels, Mary is the central character of the *Protoevangelium*. Although attributed to James "the brother of the Lord" who appears in the gospels and was a kinsman of Jesus, because of the text's apparently limited understanding of Jewish customs and Palestinian geography, it was likely written by a non-Jewish Christian or a Christian Jew who lived outside Palestine. It is a reverent and watershed work on the life of Mary, as she is cast as an exceptional child destined for great things. Her parents, a well-to-do couple named Joachim and Anna, are advanced in age and grief-stricken at their inability to conceive a child. A descendant of the royal House of David, Joachim was a righteous man of Nazareth who shared his fortune with orphans, widows, strangers and the poor. Anna was the

---

[14]   Luigi Gambero, *Mary and the Fathers of the Church: The Blessed Virgin Mary in Patristic Thought* (San Francisco: Ignatius Press, 1999) 35.

daughter of a priest of the tribe of Levi, and a native of the town of Bethlehem. Yet after a half century of living righteously before God, the couple is left with the humiliation, not uncommon in biblical Jewish culture, of dying without an heir. They both beseech God in supplication, and each receives a separate visitation from the Archangel Gabriel, who reveals to Anna that "you shall conceive and bear, and your offspring shall be spoken of in the whole world." Joachim is also visited by Gabriel, and is told that he shall conceive a daughter whose name will be Mary, and that she is to be raised in righteousness and purity "in the temple of the Lord, that it may not be possible to say, or so much as to suspect, any evil concerning her." The story follows an established biblical theme. Like such righteous figures as Abraham and Sarah and Jacob and Ruth in the Old Testament and Zachariah and Elizabeth in the gospel of Luke, Joachim and Anna appeal to the mercies of God that they might have a child, and their prayers are answered.[15]

The story of Mary's birth, childhood, and youth continues to unfold in the *Protoevangelium*, and based on the events described in it the Church eventually establishes three feast days in her honor, including her Conception (December 9), her Nativity (September 8), and her entrance into the Temple (November 21). In fulfillment of the promise her parents made to God, at the age of three Mary is taken to live in the Temple, away from the corruption of the world. There she is greeted by the high

---

[15]   James Keith Elliot, *The Apocryphal New Testament* (Oxford: Clarendon Press, 1993) 58. See also Holy Apostles Convent. *The Life of the Virgin Mary, the Theotokos*. 6.

priest, Zacharias, the future father of John the Baptist, who after embracing her prophetically proclaims, "The Lord has magnified your name among all generations; because of you the Lord at the end of days will reveal his redemption to the sons of Israel."[16]

---

[16] Holy Apostles Convent, ix, 27.

The Presentation of the Virgin in the Temple.
Russian icon, fourteenth century.

Another important stage in Mary's life not found in the gospels is presented in the *Protevangelium*. At the time she reaches puberty and begins the biological process of menstruation, according to Jewish law she must leave the Temple. The high priest Zacharias, guided by and angel, devises a plan to find a suitable husband for Mary. He accomplishes this by assembling a group of eligible widowers from the tribe of Judah, including a widowed father of seven children named Joseph. Each widower is commanded to come to the temple with his staff. Zacharias collects the walking sticks and places them in the sanctuary, where he prays intently over them, seeking a sign from the Lord that may direct him to make the best decision. After handing the rods back to each owner, a dove miraculously flies out of the top of Joseph's staff and lands on his head. The sign is given, and Joseph is chosen to be betrothed to Mary. Although he hesitates at taking such a young bride into his home, Joseph accepts the will of God, and looks after Mary.[17]

As a non-canonical work, the *Protoevangelium* is not reflective of church teaching in its entirety, although it was widely read by early Christians from the time of its appearance in the mid-second century. The purpose of the work seems to stress Mary's intact virginity before and after her betrothal to Joseph as well as her preparation of a life of holiness leading up to the birth of Jesus. The *Protoevangelium* also became a primary source for later, more speculative works about the Virgin Mary such as the *Pseudo-Gospel of Matthew*. Well respected early Christian theologians such as

---

17   Gambero, *Mary and the Fathers of the Church: The Blessed Virgin Mary in Patristic Thought*, 37-38. See also Holy Apostles Convent, 65-66.

Origen and Clement of Alexandria make reference to it, and it can be considered the foundational source after the gospels on matters related to Mary's life. Mary's parents, Joachim and Anna, are held up as exemplary role models of faithful perseverance and obedience to God. It is chiefly through the accounts of the *Protoevagelium*, while not understood in a strictly historical sense, that a fuller portrait of Mary's life is told to the Orthodox faithful.

The New Eve, the Theotokos, and the Rise of Popular Devotion to the Virgin Mary

As scholar of early Christian doctrine J.N.D. Kelly points out, from Christianity's earliest years the faithful began to venerate the martyrs of the Church, who were considered the great heroes of the faith and who through their supreme sacrifice in devotion to Christ were held in high regard and believed to already be in the glorious presence of God. At first, veneration practices began with the preservation of martyrs' relics and holding annual commemorations in their honor. As they were now with Christ in glory, Christians also began praying for their intercessory help. The great early Christian writer Origen of Alexandria (c. 185-254) defended what came to be known as the communion of saints, making the case that "the Church in heaven assists the Church on earth with its prayers." Not long after the persecution of Christians was stopped under the Roman Emperor Constantine the Great in 313, this reverence was extended to include ascetics, confessors, and other Christians leading exemplary lives of faith.[18]

Before long, the Virgin Mary was included in a distinct way among the communion of saints. Not only were oral

---

[18] J. N. D. Kelly, *Early Christian Doctrines*. (Peabody: Prince Press, 2007) 490.

traditions and written works such as the *Protoevangelium* emerging in the ante-Nicene age of the Church (100-325 C.E.), the early church fathers were also beginning to speak of her unique role in Christian salvation as well. The first to do so was St. Justin Martyr, a philosopher by training and a Christian apologist who lived in the second century and was martyred about 165. It was Justin who made one of the first known theological statements about Mary, contrasting her with Eve from the Old Testament Genesis story. While Eve chose disobedience to God leading to humanity's catastrophic fall, Mary is held up as the opposite—a role model of obedience and fidelity.[19] St. Irenaeus of Lyons (c. 130-200 C.E.) amplified this dialectic theme. Through her action of accepting God's will Mary enabled the coming of Christ, who would crush the serpent that led to humankind's ejection from the Garden. "For Adam had necessarily to be restored in Christ, that mortality be absorbed in immortality," wrote Irenaeus, "and Eve [had necessarily to be restored] in Mary, that a virgin, by becoming the advocate of a virgin, should undo and destroy virginal disobedience by virginal obedience." As Christ is the Second Adam, so too is Mary the Second Eve.[20] Any discussion of Mary is thus intertwined with Christ. As Jesus became the Incarnate Word through the freely chosen acceptance of God's will by Mary, so Mary becomes the symbolic representation of perfect discipleship to her Son.

By the third and fourth centuries, Mary's importance in relation to her Son became even more pronounced.

---

[19]   Gambero, 44-47.

[20]   Jaroslav Pelikan, *Mary Through the Centuries: Her Place in History and Culture.* (New Haven: Yale University Press, 1996) 42-43.

References to Mary as "God-bearer", or Theotokos in Greek, begin to appear in devotional prayer. The earliest surviving text of such an intercessory prayer to the Virgin was found on Egyptian papyrus and dates from the late third or early fourth centuries: "Under your mercy we take refuge, Theotokos. Do not overlook our petitions in adversity but rescue us from danger, uniquely holy one and uniquely blessed one."[21] By the fourth century the use of the term was widespread in the Church, and had been used in writings by notable patristic writers such as St. Alexander and St. Athanasius of Alexandria, as well as St. Ambrose of Milan. Renowned church historian Jaroslav Pelikan has noted that there is little doubt that "Theotokos" had been long used in popular piety even before the fourth century.[22]

Although Marian piety was spreading among the faithful, use of the term "The Mother of God" encountered dissention. Leading the opposition against the title Theotokos was Nestorius, a Syrian monk who became the Patriarch of Constantinople in 428. Nestorius objected to the use of Theotokos on the grounds that Mary did not give birth to Christ as God but rather as a man, which suggested that Christ existed as two separate persons, one human and one divine. This position ran counter to the Orthodox position held by the wider Church that the Incarnate Christ was one person who was at once God and man. St. Cyril of Alexandria led the charge against Nestorius, and won the support of Pope Celestine in the

---

[21]   Richard Price, "Theotokos: The Title and its Significance in Doctrine and Devotion". p. 56 in *Mary, The Complete Resource.* Sarah Jane Boss, ed.

[22]   Ibid. 57; Pelikan, 57-58.

West, who also condemned Nestorious' teaching. In 431, the third Ecumenical Council of the Church meeting in Ephesus condemned the Nestorian view, and proclaimed that reference to Mary as the Theotokos properly reflected and reinforced the view that Christ was both fully God and fully man. Once again, the person of Mary is inextricably tied to the person of Christ. As Marian scholar Sarah Jane Boss points out, ". . . Jesus' unique salvific power derives from his identity as both true God and true man, and for this reason Mary is central to the Christian account of God and creation."[23]

---

[23]   Ibid., 55-57. See also Price, 57-62; Jane Boss, "The Title Theotokos". p. 52 in *Mary, The Complete Resource.*Sarah Jane Boss, ed.

St. Cyril of Alexandria (c. 376-444). Early fourteenth century
fresco in the Kariye Djami, Chora Monastery in Constantinople.
Cyril's case against Nestorius in the early fifth century played an
important role in ensuring Mary's continued veneration in the
church as the *Theotokos* or Mother of God.

The Growth of the Dormition
of Mary in Christian Devotional
and Liturgical Worship

By the end of the fifth century, many of the defining characteristics concerning Mary and expressed in Orthodox Christian worship had been established within the sacred tradition of the Church: her unique and important place as Theotokos in relation to the Incarnation and two natures of Christ; her ever-virginity (to be affirmed by the Fifth Ecumenical Council at Constantinople in 553 CE); and, along with the communion of saints, her role as an intercessor and mediatrix on behalf of humanity. Indeed, this period was a time, according to Brian Daley, "of meteoric rise for the figure of Mary in popular devotion, art, and homiletics."[24] Yet the Holy Mother was to take on another, powerfully profound role in salvation history, one that would be expressed in the events surrounding her last moments on earth.

As Christians, we accept that our corporal or bodily existence is limited. Despite great advances and ongoing strides in medical research that allow us to live longer,

---

[24]   Brian Daley, "'At the Hour of Our Death': Mary's Dormition and Christian Dying in Late Patristic and Early Byzantine Literature," *Dumbarton Oaks Papers*, Vol. 55 (2001), pp. 71-89.

healthier lives, our bodies remain mortal as a consequence of the Fall of Adam and Eve. When we die, our flesh may be dead and rotting from our bones, but the salvation we have found in Christ's Resurrection gives us the supreme hope of life everlasting, and that our physical bodies will be transformed at the end of time with all of Creation. This hope, as one Orthodox catechism states, is the very foundation of Christianity, and proclaimed throughout the New Testament: "And this is the will of Him who sent Me, that everyone who sees the Son and believes in Him may have everlasting life, and I will raise him up on the last day." (John 6:40 NKJV), (cf. John 6:38-39; 2 Timothy 3:1; 1 John 2:18; Jude 1:18; 1 Peter 1:3-5). This mystical reality, as St. Matthew tells us, was evident the very day Jesus was crucified, when "the graves were opened; and many of the bodies of the saints who had fallen asleep were raised; and coming out of the graves after His resurrection, they went into the holy city [Jerusalem] and appeared to many." (Matthew 27:52-53). It is this reality we triumphantly proclaim at Pascha with "Christ is Risen!" and continue to commemorate at every divine liturgy.[25]

In addition to the biblical reality of Christ's Resurrection and Ascension into heaven, at least a few other narratives concerning the bodily assumption—or a taking up into heaven—of certain biblical figures have been present in the Hebrew scriptures, most obviously through the figures

---

[25]   George Mastratonis, A New-Style Catechism of the Eastern Orthodox Faith for Adults. (St. Louis: OLOGOS, 1977) 145. For an in-depth look at the celebration of the Eucharist and its meaning for our salvation, see Alexander Schmemann, *The Eucharist.* (Crestwood, NY: St. Vladimir's Seminary Press, 1988) 216-222.

of Enoch, the great grandson of Adam who was "taken" by God, and Prophet Elijah, who was described as being carried off to heaven in a whirlwind and accompanied by chariots.[26] Despite these scriptural references that point to the hope of a resurrected humanity, it appears that speculation on matters related to the disposition of the soul immediately after death prompted a new, popular devotion to the Theotokos as a model of Christian life and as a loving intercessor on behalf of humankind.

Although it had become generally accepted in the early Church that the great Christian martyrs who faced death courageously for their faith found themselves in Paradise at the moment of their death, it remained less clear what happened to the soul of a "typical" believer, whether a woman living with her family on an orchard farm in Cappadocia or a fisherman living on the island of Sicily. As Brian Daley points out, popular Christian perceptions of life after death in the first three centuries of Christianity were largely influenced by notions found in Jewish and Hellenistic religious culture, where the believer's best hope was to lie in a static state of comfort in the dark depths of the earth—a more restful version of Sheol or Hades—where the righteous would find rest in "the bosom of Abraham" until the time of the general resurrection of the dead at the end of history.[27]

Some relief for the faithful over the ambiguous state of the post-mortem soul was offered by the fourth century theologian St. Gregory Nazianzen, who speculated that

---

[26]   Pelikan, 207.

[27]   Daley, "'At the Hour of Our Death,': Mary's Dormition and Christian Dying in Late Patristic and Early Byzantine Literature," 74.

"every fair and God-beloved soul, when it is freed from the bonds of the body, . . . at once enjoys a sense and perception of the blessings that await it . . . and feels a wondrous pleasure and exultation, and goes rejoicing to meet its Lord." Similarly, prayers for the dead in the *Apostolic Constitutions* appearing in late fourth century Antioch point to a hopeful end, as it asks God to place the soul of the departed "in the place of the holy ones, in the bosom of Abraham, and Isaac, and Jacob, with all those who have pleased God through the ages and have done his will."[28]

But what about the state of souls of those who were far less than holy, and who must face the sins of their earthly lives, as everyone must, whether saint or sinner? Many early Church Fathers from Origen to St. Anthony of Egypt (as related in his biography by St. Anthanasius), St. Basil the Great, St. John Chrysostom, and St. John of the Ladder, among others, perceived the time immediately following death a call to purification, a final call to witness for Christ (in Greek, *martyria*) and to let go of the sins that had held them captive in their earthly life. Using the cultural references of their time, the Fathers envisioned a series of protecting angels who vied with dark angels appearing as tax collectors seeking to account for the soul's past sins. Tax collectors in the period of the Roman Empire were known for their oppressive abuse of the people. In this setting believers were to confront the many faceted sins of their past, whether rooted in pride, anger, bitterness, envy, or harmful sensory and carnal desires. These sins were encountered by the soul at a series of "toll stations" on

---

[28]   St. Gregory Nazianzen, as quoted in Daley, Ibid.

the way to ascending to heaven.[29] According to St. Cyril of Alexandria, during this final journey of purification, the departed will be protected by holy angels offering a defense of the soul's good works, eventually taking the pious and godly soul "to that ineffable joy of the blessed and eternal life."[30]

Such ancient accounts, which are part of the traditional teachings of the Church on the immediate disposition of the soul after death, likely appear to reflect, as patristic scholar Brian Daley speculates, "the unrelenting emphasis [by early Christian ascetics] on the need for penance and conversion," as well as the real prospect that judgment awaits each departing soul.[31] However by the sixth century the works of other Christian writers appear to temper the notion of angelic/demonic struggle over the soul at various "toll stations". In *The State of Souls After Death*, Eustratius of Constantinople, a sixth century priest of the great church of Hagia Sophia (Holy Wisdom), held a view that souls continue to be active after death, either praising God or working on his behalf to redeem the souls of the living.[32] However hope will also be found, once again, through the aegis of the Mother of God. It is perhaps not a coincidence that a growth in devotions to Mary as mediatrix between

---

[29]   For an exposition of the Church Father's statements on the immediate "afterdeath" experience, see "Nikolaos P. Vassiliadis, *The Mystery of Death*, Peter A. Chamberas, trans. (Athens, Greece: The Orthodox Brotherhood of Theologians "The Savior" 1993) 382-392.

[30]   Cyril of Alexandria (?), Homily 14, *On the Departure of the Soul*, and on the Second Coming (of Christ) (PG 77:1073C-1076D) as cited in Vassiliadis, p. 390.

humanity and her Son was on the rise during the same period as the promulgation of ascetic theories concerning the state of the soul after death. It is at this time as well that the story of her death and afterlife experience fully takes hold throughout the Christian Church.

The Dormition of the Mother of God.

Eastern Orthodox tradition holds that Mary died the natural death of a human being, referring to the event as the Dormition or "the falling asleep" (Greek: *kemesis*) of the Mother of God (we derive the English word "cemetery" from *kemesis*). But like her Son, Mary would not suffer bodily corruption. After a period of time, usually identified as three days, she was assumed bodily into heaven to where she dwells with her Son until the last days. While in Orthodox tradition its is generally accepted that Mary lived much of her life in Ephesus with the Apostle John, no credible archeological evidence exists to identify the precise location of Mary's death, although a shrine venerating her tomb was built in Jerusalem that scholars have evaluated to reliably indicate the existence of a tradition of Marian liturgical devotion dating back to at least the fifth century.[31] Indeed, by the early fifth century the Jerusalem church began observing the ritual feast of the Memory of Mary, which was celebrated on August 15. Within a century this feast day would be set aside exclusively to commemorate Mary's Dormition.[32]

So from where came a tradition that led to the establishment of a feast day honoring the death and assumption of Mary, and its eventual acceptance as a doctrine of the Church? Leading Marian scholar Stephen Schoemaker has identified no less that five different apocryphal narratives concerning the final days of Mary

---

[31] Stephen J. Shoemaker, "Death and the Maiden: The Early History of the Dormition and Assumption Apocrypha", *St. Vladimir's Seminary* Quarterly 60:1-2 (2006) 71.

[32] Ibid. "Marian Liturgies and Devotion in Early Christianity", in Sarah Jane Boss". p. 139, 141 in *Mary, The Complete Resource*. Sarah Jane Boss, ed.

appearing between the end of the fifth and the mid-sixth century. A Syrian narrative known as the *Book of Mary's Repose,* which survives in an Ethiopian translation, describes her bodily resurrection and its assumption or translation to Paradise.[33]

Another collection of short narratives of Syrian origin, referred to simply as the *Six Books,* provides varying details of Mary's death and the removal of her body to Paradise. The second book in this series recounts how, in her final days, Christ's apostles who were dispersed over the known world were summoned by the Holy Spirit to come to Mary's side, including some of the now dead apostles who were temporarily resurrected for the event.[34] As Mary's end on earth was approaching, she was asked by the apostles to leave the world with a final blessing, which she does, beseeching God to look after his people, and offering a litany of supplications to the Lord for the end of war, hunger, affliction, and captivity through violence, among many other things. Jesus is then heard replying to his Mother: "Everything you have said to me, Mary, I will do to please thee; and I will show mercy to everyone who calls upon thy name." When her time came, "the soul of the blessed one departed from her, and He (Jesus) sent it to the mansions of the Father's house." The apostles then prepare her body and place it on a chariot of light, to be borne by the twelve "as it went to the Paradise of Eden." Henceforth, the account goes, the apostles designated

---

[33] Shoemaker, "Death and the Maiden," 78-79.

[34] W. Wright, trans. "The Departure of My Lady Mary From This World (the *Six Books*)" in *The Journal of the Sacred Literature and Biblical Record.* VII (1865) 136-139.

specific days throughout the year to honor the Mother of God.[35]

Two other Dormition narratives of Coptic Egyptian origin, homilies loosely attributed to St. Cyril of Jerusalem and Evodius of Rome, relate a different story of Mary's fate. In these stories Mary's soul separates from her body upon her natural death, while her body miraculously disappears from her sarcophagus sometime while it was carried by the apostles during her funeral procession. In this narrative, the apostles arrive at the burial site only to discover her body missing, presumably assumed into heaven. Still another homily delivered by Jacob of Serug in 489 relates that Mary indeed died "that she might taste His [Christ's] cup," and describes the triumphal entry of Mary's soul (but not her body) into heaven. In the end, Shoemaker concludes, we must understand that the tradition of the early Dormition doctrine actually spring forth from multiple narrative sources or "archetypes"—models from which a composite narrative is based.[36]

But it is in a homily by Archbishop John of Thessalonica, delivered sometime in the early seventh century, that the story of Mary's Dormition becomes crystallized in its final form and widely referenced by the Church. It also later became the model on which the common icon of the Dormition is based. Archbishop John's tender telling of the last morning of the last day of Mary's life is moving, and is characterized more by joy than sorrow:

---

[35] Ibid., 151-153.

[36] Shoemaker, "Death and the Maiden," 80, 85; Mary Hansbury, trans. Jacob of Serug, *On the Mother of God.* (Crestwood: St. Vladimir's Seminary Press, 1998) 98-99.

And Mary got up and went outside, and raised her hands and prayed to the Lord. After her prayer she went in and lay down on her bed. Peter sat at her head and John by her feet, while the rest of the Apostles stood in a circle around her pallet. And about the third hour of the day, there was a great clap of thunder from the heavens, and a sweet fragrance, which caused all those present to be overpowered by sleep, except for the Apostles alone, and three virgins, whom the Lord appointed to stay awake so that they might be witnesses of Mary's funeral rites and her glory. And behold, the Lord came on the clouds, with a multitude of angels beyond number. And Jesus himself and Michael entered the inner chamber where Mary was, while the angels sang hymns and remained standing outside the chamber. And as soon as the savior entered, he found the Apostles with holy Mary, and he embraced them all. After this, he embraced his own mother. And Mary opened her mouth and blessed him, saying "I bless you, for you have not grieved me with regard to the things you foretold. You foretold that you would not allow angels to come again to seek my soul, but that you would come for it yourself. It has happened, Lord, according to your word (cf. Luke: 1:38). Who am I, lowly one, that I have been counted worthy of such glory?" And having said this, she brought the course of her life to its fulfillment, her face turned smilingly towards the Lord. And the Lord took her soul and placed it in the hands of Michael, after wrapping it in veils of some kind, whose splendor it is impossible to describe.[37]

---

[37] John, Archbishop of Thessalonica. "The Dormition of Our Lady, the Mother of God and Ever-Virgin Mary", in Brian

With the help of questions put to Christ by the apostle Peter, the narrative continues with what amounts to an explanation of the significance of Mary's Dormition for humanity:

> The Apostles looked on as the soul of Mary was given into the hands of Michael, filled out with all the members of human being, except for the form of female and male, but with nothing else in it except the likeness of the whole body and a brilliance seven times greater than the sun. Peter was filled with joy, and asked the Lord, "Is the soul of each of us bright, as Mary's is?" The Lord said to him, "O Peter, the souls of all those being born in this world are like this, but when they depart from the body they are not in such a brilliant condition, because they were sent here in one state and later found in another. For 'they loved the darkness' (Jn. 3:19) of many sins. *But if someone guards himself from the inequities of this world's darkness, and so leaves the body, his soul will be found to be as bright as this.*" (Author's italics)[38]

John's account concludes with the story of the Apostles' surprise when they returned to Mary's tomb on the third day after her passing to find only her burial garments, her body having been taken to be in Paradise with her Son. Following John of Thessalonica, many other Church Fathers, including St. Modestos of Jerusalem, St. Andrew of Crete, St. Germanos of Constantinople, and

---

E. Daley, S.J., trans. *On the Dormition of Mary: Early Patristic Homilies* (Crestwood: St. Vladimir's Seminary Press, 1998) 62-63.

[38] Ibid., 63.

St. Theodore the Studite, wrote extensively concerning the doctrine. By the eighth century the Dormition/Assumption theme was firmly rooted in the worship life of the Church and eloquently praised in song by the last of the great Early Church Fathers, St. John of Damascus:

> Come here, good friends, let us celebrate,
> With all of God's faithful and holy ones,
> Mary's great festival;
> Come, sing to Christ, who was born of her,
> Clapping our hands to praise him:
> Glory to both of them!
> From you the flower of life sprang forth,
> Not bursting the gates of your virginity;
> Source of vitality,
> How could your temple immaculate
> Ever be made to share in
> Death's dissolution?
> You sheltered life as its sanctuary;
> Now life without end is your inheritance,
> Life is your dwelling-place.
> Crossing this river mortality,
> You who call life your offspring,
> Share his eternity.[39]

---

[39]   John of Damascus, "Canon for the Dormition of the Mother of God (Tone IV)" in Brian E. Daley, S.J. trans. *On the Dormition of Mary: Early Patristic Homilies*, 243-244.

St. John of Damascus (c.676-749). Early fourteenth century fresco from the tombs in the Kariye Djami, Chora Monastery in Constantinople.

The Hope of Humanity

After more than 1,600 years of development within the Sacred Tradition of the Church, Eastern Orthodox Christians continue to strongly affirm and proclaim Mary's bodily assumption into Paradise *following* her death, just as her Son tasted death before his Glorious Resurrection on the third day. In North America alone, sixty-five Orthodox Christian churches (including one cathedral) and three monasteries, are named in honor of the Dormition of the Theotokos. However, unlike the Roman Catholic Church, the Orthodox Church found it unnecessary to formally pronounce the church's teachings regarding the death and assumption of the Theotokos as an official dogma. According to Kallistos Ware, the glorification of Mary doesn't belong to the Church's public preaching but rather emerges from its "inner Tradition." The great twentieth century Orthodox theologian Vladimir Lossky holds that doctrinal statements about the Mother of God are "not so much an object of faith as a foundation of our hope, a fruit of faith ripened by Tradition."[40]

It appears likely that the doctrine of Mary's Dormition and her glorious Assumption into the presence of her Son evolved within the broader Tradition of the Church as a teachable narrative to reaffirm the hope of God's eternal love. As such, the doctrine has less to do with the veracity of the historic events it reports but rather has much more

---

[40]   Ware, 265.

to do with the development of the traditions of devotion and worship from which it sprang. It is a doctrine founded upon the *experiential, existential needs of the faithful,* and one that was further enriched through the iconography and hymnography of the Church.

As she has accomplished through her role as the Ever-Virgin, Theotokos, and Mediatrix, Mary through her Dormition and Assumption provides the faithful yet another portal to her Son Jesus, who we believe destroyed the bondage of death when he descended into Hades at the time of his Resurrection. One Marian scholar perhaps summed it up best in her observation that "speech about Mary is, in the end, speech about redeemed humanity."[41] The great twentieth century Orthodox Theologian Fr. Alexander Schmemann perhaps put it best when considering the significance of the falling asleep of the Mother of God for Christians:

> In the Dormition, the whole joyful mystery of this [Mary's] death is revealed to us and becomes our joy, for Mary the Virgin Mother is one of us. If death is the horror and grief of separation, of descent into terrible loneliness and darkness, then none of this is present in the death of the Virgin Mary, since her death, like her entire life, is all encounter, all love, all continuous movement toward the unfading, never-setting light of eternity and entrance into it. "Perfect love casts out fear," says John the Theologian, the apostle of love (1 John 4:18). And therefore there is no fear in the deathless falling asleep of

---

[41]   Elizabeth A. Johnson, "The Symbolic Character of Theological Statements About Mary," *Journal of Ecumenical Studies,* 22:2, Spring 1985, 312.

the Virgin Mary. Here, death is conquered from within, freed with all that fills it with horror and hopelessness. Death itself becomes triumphant life. [42]

Although through the lens of our modern day, empirically-centered, post-modern world some would be tempted to view the doctrine of the Dormition as a fanciful tale of late antiquity, for Orthodox Christians the Glorious Dormition and Assumption of the Ever-Virgin, Mother of God remains a richly symbolic but real manifestation of God's abiding love and desire for the salvation of all his people. It is in this spirit of hope in the Lord's mercy that that we prayerfully proclaim and supplicate to his Holy Mother during the Vespers of the Feast:

> With what lips shall we, poor and worthless, call the Theotokos blessed? She is more honored than the creation, and more holy than the cherubim and all the angels . . .
>
> For by thy deathless Dormition thou has sanctified the whole world, and then hast been translated to the places above the world, there to perceive the beauty of the Almighty. Thou art attended by ranks of angels, O pure Virgin, and by the souls of the just. Join them to ask for us peace and great mercy.[44]

~ AMEN ~

---

[42] Alexander Schmemann, *The Virgin Mary: Celebration of Faith, Vol. 3*, John A. Jillions, trans. (Crestwood, NY: St. Vladimir's Seminary Press, 1995) 41.

"Theotokos the Life-Giving Font" is an iconographic representation of the Virgin and Christ Child based on a miracle that occurred in fifth-century Constantinople at the site where a church would later be built. The "living water" is analogous to Christ. Stained glass rendition. Assumption Greek Orthodox Church, St. Louis, Missouri.

Appendix:
Hymnography for the Commemoration of the Falling Asleep of our Most Holy Lady, the Mother of God and Ever-Virgin Mary.

Adapted with permission from the translation of
Archimandrite Ephrem Lash
http://www.anastasis.org.uk/15aug.htm

SMALL VESPERS

At Lord, I have cried we insert 4 Stichera, doubling the 1st.

Tone 2.

With what lips may we, poor and worthless, call the Mother of God blessed? She is greater in honor than creation and holier than the Cherubim and all the Angels; the unshakeable throne of the King; the house in which the Most High made his dwelling; the salvation of the world; the Sanctuary of God; on her memorial she richly grants to all the faithful his great mercy. *(Twice)*

What songs of awe did all the Apostles of the Word offer you then, O Virgin, as they stood around your deathbed and cried out with amazement: 'The King's palace is being taken up. The Ark of sanctification is being exalted.

Be lifted up, you gates, that the Gate of God may enter with great joy, as without ceasing she asks his great mercy for the world'?

What spiritual songs may we now offer you, O All-holy? For by your immortal Falling Asleep you have sanctified the whole world and have passed over to regions beyond the world to contemplate the beauty of the Almighty and to rejoice with him as his Mother. Angelic ranks and the souls of the Righteous escort you, pure Virgin. With them ask peace for us and his great mercy.

Glory to the Father and to the Son and to the Holy Spirit, now and ever and unto the ages of ages. Amen.

Tone 2.

She who is higher than the heavens, more glorious than the Cherubim and greater in honor than all creation, who through her surpassing purity became the vessel of the eternal being, today places in the hands of her Son her all-holy soul. With her the universe is filled with joy and to us is given his great mercy.

At the Aposticha. Tone 2.

Having come from the ends of the earth at an all-powerful command, the company of the Disciples is gathering to bury the Mother who gave birth to God.

Verse: Arise, Lord, to your rest; you and the Ark of your sanctification.

The Bride of God, the Queen and Virgin, the glory of the elect and pride of Virgins, is passing over to her Son.

51

Verse: The Lord has sworn truth to David and will not annul it: Of the fruit of your womb I will place on your throne.

The choir of Disciples has been marvelously gathered from the ends of the world to bury your divine and most pure body.

Glory to the Father and to the Son and to the Holy Spirit, now and ever and unto the ages of ages. Amen.

Gracious Lady, raise your holy hands towards your Son, the Fashioner and Lover of souls, that he may take pity on your servants.

Apolytikion. Tone 1.

In giving birth you retained your virginity; in falling asleep, O Mother of God, you did not abandon the world. You passed over into life, you, the Mother of life; and by your prayers you deliver our souls from death.

Dismissal.

GREAT VESPERS

We recite the 1st Section of the 1st Kathisma, "Blessed is the man." At "Lord, I have cried" we insert 8 Stichera.

Tone 1.

O marvelous wonder! The source of life is laid in a grave, and the tomb becomes a ladder to heaven. Be glad,

O Gethsemane, the holy shrine of the Mother of God. Let us the faithful cry, with Gabriel as our captain: O Full of grace, hail! The Lord is with you, who grants the world through you his great mercy. *(Three times)*.

O wonder of your mysteries, pure Lady! You were proclaimed the Throne of the Most High, and you have passed today from earth to heaven. Your glory is full of splendor, shining with grace in divine brightness. O Virgins, with the Mother of the King, be raised to the heights. O Full of grace, hail! The Lord is with you, who grants the world through you his great mercy. *(Three times)*.

Dominions, Thrones, Rulers, Principalities and Powers, Cherubim and the fearful Seraphim glorify your Falling Asleep. Those born of earth rejoice, adorned by your divine glory. Kings fall down and sing with Angels and Archangels: O Full of grace, hail! The Lord is with you, who grants the world through you his great mercy. *(Twice)*

Glory to the Father and to the Son and to the Holy Spirit, now and ever and unto the ages of ages. Amen.

Tone 1.

By divine command the god-bearing Apostles were caught up from all over the world by clouds on high.

Tone 5.

Reaching your all-immaculate body, source of life, they kissed it with mighty honor.

Tone 2.

The highest Powers of heaven stood by with their own Master.

Tone 6.

Seized with dread they accompanied your inviolate body that had contained God; while they went on before in a manner not of this world in crying out, unseen, to the ranks above them: See, the Queen of all, God's Child, has come.

Tone 3.

Lift up the gates, and in a manner not of this world receive the Mother of the everlasting light.

Tone 7.

For through her the salvation of all mortals has come. We have not the strength to gaze on her, and it is not possible to render her worthy honor.

Tone 4.

For her excellence outstrips all understanding.

Tone 8.

Therefore, immaculate Mother of God, as you live forever with the life-bearing King, your Offspring, pray without ceasing that he guard and save from every hostile assault your new people; for we have gained your protection.

Tone 1.

As to the ages with splendor we call you blessed.

Entrance, O Joyful Light. Prokeimenon of the day
and the Readings.
The Reading is from Genesis.
[28:10-17]

Jacob went out from the well of the oath and journeyed towards Harran. And he lighted on a place and slept there, for the sun had set. And he took one of the stones of the place and put it at his head; and he slept in that place, and he dreamed. And behold, a ladder set up on the earth, whose head reached to heaven; and the Angels of God were going up and going down upon it. But the Lord stood above it and said: 'I am the God of Abraham, your father, and the God of Isaac, do not be afraid. The land on which you are sleeping I shall give to you and to your seed. And your seed will be like the sand of the earth, and it will be spread abroad to the Sea and Liva and North and East; and in you and in your seed all the tribes of the earth will be blessed. And behold, I am with you, guarding you on every road on which you may journey; and I shall bring you back again to this land, because I shall never abandon you until I have done all that I have said to you'. And Jacob arose from his sleep and said: 'The Lord is in this place, but I did not know it'. And he was afraid, and said: 'How fearful is this place! This is none other than the house of God, this is the gate of heaven'.

The Reading is from the Prophecy of Ezekiel.
[43:72, 44:1]

'It shall be from the eighth day and upwards, the Priests shall make your holocausts upon the altar, and those for your salvation; and I shall accept you', says the Lord. And he turned me back by the way of the outer gate of the Holy Place, which looks towards the east, and it was shut. And the Lord said to me: 'This gate shall be shut, it shall not be opened, and no one shall pass through it, because the Lord, the God of Israel, will enter through it, and it shall be shut. Therefore this prince shall sit in it to eat bread. By the way of the Elam of the gate he shall enter, and by that way he shall go out'. And he brought me by the way of the gate towards the North, opposite the House; and I saw, and behold the whole house of the Lord was full of glory.

The Reading is from Proverbs.
[9:1-11]

Wisdom has built herself a house. She has slaughtered her beasts and mixed her wine in the mixing bowl, and prepared her table. She her sent out her servants, to invite with a loud proclamation upon the mixing bowl: 'Whoever is foolish, let him turn to me'. And to those who lack wisdom she said: 'Come, eat my bread, and drink the wine that I have mixed for you. Abandon folly, and you will live; and seek understanding that you may have life, and set aright your understanding with knowledge. One who corrects the wicked will gain dishonor for himself. One who rebukes the impious will get blame for himself; for to the impious rebukes are blows. Do not rebuke the wicked, lest they hate you. Rebuke a wise man and he will love you. Give instruction to a wise man and he will be wiser; teach a just man and he will increase learning. The beginning of wisdom is the fear of the Lord, and the counsel of Saints, understanding. While to know the law is the part of a good mind. For by this means you will live for a long time, and years will be added to your life'.

At the Liti, Idiomel Stichera.

Tone 1.

It was fitting for the eye-witnesses and ministers of the Word to see the Falling Asleep of his Mother according to the flesh, the final mystery concerning her, that they might not only see the Ascension of the Savior from the earth, but also be witnesses to the Translation from earth of her who bore him. Therefore, carried over from all parts by divine power, they came to Zion and escorted her, as she who is higher than the Cherubim hastened towards heaven. With them we worship her as she intercedes for our souls.

Tone 2. By Anatolios.

She who is higher than the heavens, more glorious than Cherubim and greater in honor than creation, who through her surpassing purity became the vessel of the eternal being, today places in the hands of her Son her all-holy soul. With her the universe is filled with joy and to us is given his great mercy.

The same Tone. By John.

The all-blameless Bride and Mother of the Father's Good Pleasure, who was foreordained by God as a dwelling for himself of the union without confusion, today delivers her immaculate soul to her Maker and God. The Bodiless Powers receive her in a manner fitting God, and she, who is indeed Mother of life, passes over to life, the lamp of the unapproachable Light, the salvation of the faithful, the hope of our souls.

Tone 3. By Germanos.

Come, all the ends of the earth, let us call blessed the Translation of the Mother of God. For she has placed her unblemished soul in the hands of her Son. Therefore the world has been restored to life by her holy Falling Asleep, as with psalms and hymns and spiritual songs it radiantly celebrates the feast with the Bodiless hosts and the Apostles.

Glory to the Father and to the Son and to the Holy Spirit, now and ever and unto the ages of ages. Amen.

Tone 5. By Theophanes.

Come, gathering of the lovers of festivals; come, and let us form a choir; come, let us garland the Church with songs as the Ark of God goes to her rest. For today heaven unfolds its bosom as it receives the one who gave birth to him whom nothing can contain. The earth, as it gives back the source of life, is robed in blessing and majesty. Angels with Apostles form a choir as they gaze with fear while she who gave birth to the Prince of life is translated from life to life. Let us all worship her as we beg: 'Sovereign Lady, do not forget your ties of kinship with those who celebrate with faith your all-holy Falling Asleep'.

Now and ever and unto the ages of ages. Amen. Same Tone.

Sing, you peoples, to the Mother of our God, sing! For today she places her soul, all filled with light, in the immaculate palms of the One who was incarnate from her without seed. And she implores him without ceasing that to the inhabited world there may be granted his peace and great mercy.

At the Aposticha. Tone 4.

Come, you peoples, let us sing the praises of the pure, all-holy Virgin, from whom the Word of the Father came forth ineffably incarnate, as we cry and say: Blessed are you among women. Blessed is the womb which contained Christ. As you deliver your soul into his holy hands, intercede, O Immaculate, that our souls may be saved.

Verse: Rise, Lord, to your rest; you and the Ark of your sanctification.

The multitudes of Angels in heaven and we the human race on earth call your all-revered Falling Asleep blessed, O pure and all-holy Virgin; because you became Mother of the Maker of all things, Christ God. Do not cease to intercede with him, we beg, for us who next to God place our hopes in you, O Mother of God, all-praised and who did not know wedlock.

Verse: The Lord has sworn truth to David, and will not annul it: Of the fruit of your womb I will place on your throne.

You peoples, let us sing David's song today to Christ God: 'Virgins, he says, will be brought after her to the King, they will be brought in joy and gladness'. For she, who is from the seed of David and through whom we have been made divine, passes over in glory and beyond reason into the hands of her own Son and Master. As we sing her praise as Mother of God we cry out and say: 'Save us who confess you, O Mother of God, from every disaster, and from dangers rescue our souls'.

Glory to the Father and to the Son and to the Holy Spirit, now and ever and unto the ages of ages. Amen.

Tone 4.

When you departed, Virgin Mother of God, to the One who was born ineffably from you, James, God's brother and first Hierarch, was present with Peter, the most honored high summit of the Theologians, and all the godly choir of the Apostles; in teachings that revealed the things of God they sang in praise of the divine and amazing mystery of Christ's dispensation; and as they buried your body, source of life and which had received God, O all-praised, they rejoiced. From above the all-holy and most venerable of the Angelic Powers, amazed at the wonder, bowed and said to one another: 'Lift up your gates and receive her who gave birth to the Maker of heaven and earth. And let us praise with hymns of glory the revered and holy body which contained the Lord on whom we may not look'. Therefore we too, as we celebrate your memory, cry out to you, all-praised: 'Exalt the horn of Christians and save our souls'.

Apolytikion. Tone 1.

In giving birth you retained your virginity; in falling asleep, O Mother of God, you did not abandon the world.

You passed over into life, you, the Mother of life; and by your prayers you deliver our souls from death.

Dismissal.

MATINS

After the 1st Reading from the Psalter, Kathisma.

Tone 4.

David, cries out: 'What is this present feast? The one I sang of in the book of Psalms, he says, as daughter and child of God and Virgin, Christ, who was born from her without seed, has taken over to the mansions of the world to come; and therefore mothers and daughters and brides of Christ rejoice as they cry: Hail, you who have passed over into the palaces on high'.

Glory to the Father and to the Son and to the Holy Spirit, now and ever and unto the ages of ages. Amen.

The same.

After the 2nd Reading, Kathisma.

Tone 1.

The all-honored choir of the wise Apostles was wondrously assembled to bury with glory your immaculate body, O all-praised Mother of God. With them the multitudes of Angels also raised their song as they reverently praised your Translation, which we celebrate with faith.

Glory to the Father and to the Son and to the Holy Spirit, now and ever and unto the ages of ages. Amen.

The same.

After the Polyeleos, Kathisma.

Tone 3.

In your giving birth conception was without seed; in your falling asleep death was without corruption. A double wonder ran to meet a wonder, O Mother of God; for how could one who knew not wedlock suckle a babe, while yet remaining pure? How could God's Mother be carried as a corpse while yet giving off sweet fragrance? And so with the Angel we cry to you: 'Hail, full of grace!'

Glory to the Father and to the Son and to the Holy Spirit, now and ever and unto the ages of ages. Amen.

The same. Prokeimenon.

Tone 4.

I will remember your name from generation to generation.

Verse: Listen, O daughter, see and incline your ear; and forget your people and your father's house.

After the Gospel and Psalm 50:

Glory to the Father and to the Son and to the Holy Spirit.

At the prayers of the Mother of God, O Merciful, wipe out the multitude of my transgressions.

Now and ever and unto the ages of ages. Amen.

At the prayers of the Mother of God, O Merciful, wipe out the multitude of my transgressions.

Have mercy on me, O God, according to your great mercy; and according to the multitude of your compassions wipe away my offense.

Then the Sticheron for Psalm 50.

Tone 6. By Vyzas.

When the Translation of your pure Body was being prepared, the Apostles surrounded your deathbed and looked on you with dread. And as they gazed at your body they were seized with awe, while Peter cried out to you with tears: 'Immaculate Virgin, I see you, who are the life of all, lying here outstretched, and I am struck with wonder; for in you the Delight of the life to come made his dwelling. But fervently implore your Son and God that your City may be kept safe from harm'.

Then the two Canons are sung. The 1st in Tone 1, with the Irmi, to 8 and the 2nd in Tone 4, with the Irmi, to 6. Finally the Irmi again as Katavsias.

First Canon.

A Composition by Kyr Kosmas.

Ode 1. Tone 1. Irmos.

Your sacred and renowned memorial, embroidered, O Virgin, with divine glory, has brought all the faithful together

63

for joy and led by Miriam with dances and timbrels they sing to your Only-begotten Son, for he has been glorified.

Troparia

A host of the immaterial dwellers in heaven was attending your godlike body in Zion; while suddenly the multitude of the Apostles, streaming together from the ends of the earth, stood beside you all at once, Mother of God; with them, immaculate Virgin, we glorify your august memory.

You have carried off prizes of victory against nature, Pure Virgin, in bearing God; yet, imitating your Maker and Son, beyond nature you submit to nature's laws; and so dying, you rise with your Son and live forever.

Second Canon.

A Composition by John of Damascus.

Ode 1. Tone 4. Irmos.

I will open my mouth and it will be filled with the Spirit, and I will utter a word for the Queen and Mother, and I will be seen keeping glad festival, and rejoicing I will sing her falling Asleep.

Troparia

Young virgin maidens with Miriam the Prophetess, now raise the song of departure; for the Virgin and only Mother of God is being taken over to her appointed place in heaven.

The divine tabernacles of heaven fittingly received you as a living heaven, all-pure Virgin; and as a blameless bride you stand radiantly adorned before your King and God.

Ode 3. Irmos.

O Christ, the Wisdom and Power of God, which creates and upholds all, establish the Church unshaken and unwavering; for you alone are holy, who have your resting place among the Saints.

Troparia

Knowing you, All-blameless, to be a mortal woman, but beyond nature Mother of God, with fearful hands the illustrious Apostles touched you, as you blazed with glory, gazing on you as the Tabernacle that had received God.

Just punishment intervened to cut off the sacrilegious hands of the presumptuous, for God guarded with the glory of the godhead the reverence due to the living Ark, in which the Word had become flesh.

Second Canon. Irmos.

O Mother of God, as a living and unstinted fount, establish those united in spiritual fellowship who sing you hymns of praise, and in your divine glory grant them crowns of glory.

Troparia

Pure Virgin, sprung from mortal loins, your final departure was in conformity with nature; but, as you gave birth to the true life, you have passed over to the one who is the divine life in person.

A company of Theologians from the ends of the earth and a multitude of Angels hastened to Zion at an all-powerful command, that they might fittingly minister at your burial, Sovereign Lady.

Tone 5.

All generations we call you blessed, Virgin Mother of God; for in you Christ our God, the uncontainable, was well-pleased to be contained. Blessed are we also, for we have your protection, for day and night you intercede for us and the scepters of the kingdom are strengthened by your intercessions. And so we sing your praises and cry out to you: 'Hail, full of grace, the Lord is with you'.

Ode 4. Irmos.

The sayings and riddles of the Prophets foreshadowed your incarnation from a Virgin, O Christ, even the brightness of your lightning, which would come as a light for the nations; and the deep calls to you with joy: Glory to your power, O Lover of mankind.

Troparia

See, you peoples, and marvel; for the holy and most manifest mountain of God is being lifted up far above the hills of heaven, as the earthly heaven makes her dwelling in a heavenly and incorruptible land.

Death has become for you, pure Virgin, a crossing to an eternal and better life, translating you from one which perishes to one which is truly divine and without change, to gaze in joy upon your Son and Lord.

The gates of heaven were lifted up, the Angels sang in praise and Christ received the virgin treasure of his own Mother. Cherubim withdrew before you with gladness and Seraphim glorify you with joy.

Second Canon. Irmos.

The prophet Avvakoum, perceiving the unsearchable divine counsel of your incarnation from the Virgin, O Most High, cried out: Glory to your power, O Lord!

Troparia

Strange marvel it was to see the living heaven of the universal King going down below the hollows of the earth. How wonderful are your works! Glory to your power, O Lord!

At your Translation, Mother of God, the hosts of Angels in fear and joy covered with hallowed wings your body that had been spacious enough to receive God.

If her fruit, who is beyond understanding, because of whom she was called Heaven, willingly underwent burial as a mortal, how will she refuse burial, who bore him without wedlock?

Ode 5. Irmos.

I shall expound the divine and ineffable beauty of your virtues, O Christ; for you shone out from the eternal glory as the empersonned and eternal brightness, and taking flesh, and incarnate from a virgin womb, for those in darkness and in shadow you dawned as the sun'.

Troparia

Riding as though upon a cloud, the company of the Apostles was being gathered to Zion from the ends of the earth to minister, O Virgin, to you, the light cloud, from which God the Most High, the Sun of righteousness had shone for those in darkness.

The inspired tongues of men who were theologians, resonant with the Spirit, cried out more loudly than trumpets the burial hymn for the Mother of God: Hail, unsullied source of God's incarnation, origin of life and salvation for all.

Second Canon. Irmos.

The universe was amazed at your divine glory, for you, O Virgin, who did not know wedlock, have passed over from earth to eternal mansions and to life without end, as you give salvation as the prize to all who sing your praise.

Troparia

Let the trumpets of the theologians ring out today, and let the human tongue now sound praises with many voices. Let the air re-echo, shining with infinite light. Let Angels honor with hymns the Falling Asleep of the Virgin.

The vessel of election, wholly beside himself, wholly transported, surpassed himself in hymns to you, O Virgin; wholly consecrated to God, he truly was and proved himself to all to be possessed by God, O all-praised Mother of God.

Ode 6. Irmos.

The fire within the whale, the monster dwelling in the sea, was a prefiguring of your three-day burial; and Jonas acted as interpreter, for saved and unharmed, as though he had never been swallowed, he cried aloud: I will sacrifice to you with a voice of praise, O Lord!

Troparia

The Suzerain and God of all apportions to you the things above nature; for just as he kept you a Virgin in your giving birth, so he preserved your body incorrupt in the tomb, and he glorified you with him by a divine Translation, gracing you with honors, as a Son his Mother.

Your Offspring, O Virgin, has truly made you dwell in the Holy of Holies as shining Lampstand of the immaterial fire, golden Censer of the divine coal, Jar and Rod and Tablet written by God, holy Ark and Table of the bread of life.

Second Canon. Irmos.

As we celebrate this divine and honored feast of the Mother of God, come, godly-minded people, let us clap our hands as we glorify God who was born of her.

Life dawned from you without loosing the keys of your virginity. How then has your spotless tabernacle, source of life, become a partaker in the experience of death?

Once the sacred enclosure of life, you have found eternal life; for through death you, who gave birth to life in person, have passed over to life.

Kontakion. Tone 2.

Nor tomb nor death overpowered the Mother of God, unsleeping in her prayers, unfailing hope in intercession; for as Mother of Life she has been taken over to life by him who dwelt in her ever-virgin womb.

Ikos

Set a rampart about my mind, my Savior, for I dare to sing the praise of the rampart of the world, your all-pure Mother. Strengthen me in the tower of my words and fortify my in the turrets of my thoughts. For you cry out that you fulfill the requests of those who ask in faith. Grant me therefore tongue, utterance and thought without shame. For every gift of enlightenment is sent down from you, Giver of light, who dwelt in her ever-virgin womb.

Synaxarion

On the 15th of the month, commemoration of the all-revered Translation of our most glorious Lady and ever-virgin Mary.

Verses.

No wonder that the Maiden, world's salvation, dies.
When the world's Fashioner in the flesh had died,
God's Mother ever lives, though the fifteenth she died.

When Christ our God was well pleased to take to himself his own Mother, three days before he told her through an Angel of her translation from the earth. It is the moment, he said, to take my Mother to myself. Do not then be any way troubled by this, but accept my word with joy, for you are coming to immortal life. And she, in her longing for her translation to her Son, went up the mount of Olives with haste to pray (for it was her custom to go up there to pray). Then there took place a marvel; for the plants on the mount bowed themselves down of their own accord and like living slaves accomplished fitting reverence to their Lady. After her prayer she returned home and at once the whole house was shaken. She prepared many lights and having given thanks to God she invited her relatives and neighbors. She swept the house and prepared the couch and everything needed for the burial. She explained everything which had been told her by the Angel about her translation to heaven and as confirmation of her words showed the reward that had been given her, which was a palm branch [from Paradise]. But the women who had been summoned on hearing this poured out lamentations and tears and lamented with cries of grief. When they ceased their lament they begged her not to leave them orphans. She assured them that when she had passed over she would watch over and protect not only them but the whole world. Much of their grief was assuaged by these words of consolation which she spoke to the bystanders. Then she gave instructions about her two tunics, that the two poor widows who were customarily with her and known to her and who received from her what was required for their nourishment should take one each.

While she was detailing and arranging this, there suddenly came the sound of mighty thunder and the arrival of many clouds from the ends of the earth bringing Christ's disciples together to the house of God's Mother. Among them also were the Hierarchs, wise in God, Denys the Areopagite, Hierothoes and Timothy. When they learned the reason of their presence together they spoke to her as follows: While we saw you, Lady, remaining in the world, like our Master and Teacher himself, we were comforted; but how shall we now bear the suffering? But since by the wish of your Son and God you are passing over to the regions beyond the world, we rejoice for the things that have been so disposed for you. As they said this they wept profusely. But she answered them: Friends and Disciples of my Son and God, do not turn my joy to sorrow, but bury my body just as I have arranged it on the bed.

When these things had been completed, Paul the inspired vessel of election arrived. He fell at the feet of God's Mother, worshipped and opening his mouth uttered a great eulogy of her, saying: Hail, Mother of life and subject of my preaching. For though I never saw Christ, in seeing you I seem to see him. Then the Virgin took leave of all. She lay down on the bed and arranged her all-pure body as she wished. She prayed for the conservation of the world and for peaceful life. She filled them too with blessing through her, and so committed her spirit into the hands of her own Son and God.

At this Peter began the funeral hymns. The rest of the Apostles took up the bier and accompanied the body that had received God to the grave, some going in front with lamps and hymns, others following behind. At this the rulers of the Jews stirring up some of the crowd persuaded them to try to upset the bier on which the life-giving body had been placed and to throw it to the ground. But already punishment came upon those who dared such things, and they were all smitten with blindness. One of them, who attempting even greater folly had touched the sacred bier, was deprived of both his insolent hands. They were severed by the sword of punishment and left hanging from the bier. He remained a pitiable sight until, after he had come to belief with his whole heart and found healing, he was restored to health as before. So too part of the covering of the bier, when placed on those who had been blinded and come to belief, gave them healing. When the Apostles reached Gethsemane they laid the live-giving body in the grave and remained there for three days responding to the unceasing voices of the Angels.

But when, by divine dispensation, one of the Apostles, who had been absent from the burial of the life-giving body, arrived on the third day, he was greatly grieved and distressed that he had not been found worthy of what they had. All his fellow Apostles, who had been found worthy, by a common vote opened the tomb for the sake of the Apostle who had been absent, so it seemed good to all, for him also to venerate that all-blameless body. When they looked they were amazed. For they found it empty of the holy body, and containing only the winding sheet, which remained as a consolation for those who were about to grieve and for all the faithful, and as a sure witness of the Translation. For even until today the tomb hewn from the rock is visible and venerated, and remains empty of a body, to the glory and honor of our most blessed Lady, Mother of God and ever-virgin Mary.

At whose holy intercessions, O God, have mercy and save us, as you are good and love mankind.

Ode 7. Irmos.

Fighting against cruel wrath and fire, love divine quenched the fire with dew, and laughed the wrath to scorn, making the three-stringed lyre of the Saints, inspired by God, sing in the midst of the flame, in answer to the instruments of music: Blessed are you, most glorious God, our God and the God of our fathers.

Troparia

In wrath Moses smashed the tablets made by God, written by the divine Spirit; but his Master having kept her who gave him birth unharmed for heavenly abodes, has now made her dwell in them. As with her we leap for joy, we cry to Christ: Blessed are you, most glorious God, our God and the God of our fathers.

With cymbals of pure lips and the harmonious harp of the heart, with the well-sounding trumpet of an uplifted mind, as we clap with active hands, we cry on this auspicious and chosen day of the translation of the pure Virgin: Blessed are you, most glorious God, our God and the God of our fathers.

The people inspired by God has gathered; for the Tabernacle of God's glory is being translated in Zion to a heavenly abode, where there is the pure sound of those who feast, the voice of ineffable joy of those who cry with gladness to Christ: Blessed are you, most glorious God, our God and the God of our fathers.

Second Canon. Irmos.

The godlike Youths did not worship creation instead of the Creator, but bravely trampling on the threat of fire, rejoicing they sang: O highly exalted Lord and God of our fathers, blessed are you!

Troparia

Young men and maidens, old men and rulers, kings with judges, as you honor the memory of the Virgin and Mother of God, sing out: Lord and God of our fathers, blessed are you!

Let the mountains of heaven resound with the trumpet of the Spirit; let hills now rejoice, and let the godlike Apostles leap for joy: the Queen is being translated to her Son, with who she rules for ever.

The most sacred Translation of your godlike and undefiled Mother has gathered the celestial ranks of the Powers on high to rejoice together with those on earth who sing to you: O God, blessed are you!

Ode 8. Irmos.

The all-powerful Angel of God revealed to the Youths a flame that brought refreshment to the Holy, but consumed the ungodly; while he made the Mother of God a spring, source of life, gushing forth the destruction of death, but life for those who sing: We who have been delivered praise the only Creator, and highly exalt him to all the ages.

Troparia

The whole multitude of the Divines accompanied the Ark of God in Zion with words, as they cried: Where do you now depart, Tabernacle of the living God? Do not cease to watch over those who sing: We who have been delivered praise the only Creator, and highly exalt him to all the ages.

As she departed the All-blameless lifted up her hands, which had held God incarnate in their embrace, and she said with a Mother's boldness to the One whom she had borne: Those whom you have made mine keep unto the ages, as they cry to you: We who have been delivered praise the only Creator, and highly exalt him to all the ages.

Second Canon. Irmos.

The Offspring of the Mother of God saved the innocent Youths in the furnace. Then he was prefigured, but now in reality he gathers the whole world which sings: All you works, praise the Lord, and highly exalt him to all the ages.

Troparia

Immaculate Virgin, Rulers and Dominions with Powers, Angels, Archangels, Thrones, Principalities, the Cherubim and the dread Seraphim glorify your memory; while we, the human race, praise and highly exalt you to all the ages.

He, who when taking flesh made his dwelling strangely in your immaculate womb, himself received your all-holy spirit and, as a dutiful Son, gave it rest with himself. And so we praise you, O Virgin, and exalt you above all to all the ages.

Ode 9.

Megalynarion, which is sung before each Troparion of the following Ode:

All generations call you blessed, the only Mother of God.

Irmos.

In you, O Virgin without spot, the bounds of nature have been overcome; for childbirth remains virgin, and death is betrothed to life; Virgin after bearing child, and alive after death, O Mother of God, may you ever save your inheritance.

The angelic Powers were amazed as they looked in Zion on their own Master bearing in his hands the soul of a woman; for as befitted a Son he was saying to the one who gave him birth without spot: Come, honored Lady, be glorified with your Son and God.

The choir of the Apostles shrouded your Body, which had received God, as they looked with awe and addressed you with clear voice: As you depart into heavenly bridal chambers to your Son, may you ever save your inheritance.

Second Canon.

Megalynarion, sung as the one above:

Angels, when they saw the falling Asleep of the Virgin, were amazed at how the Virgin went up from earth to the things on high.

The angelic Powers were amazed as they looked in Zion on their own Master bearing in his hands the soul of a woman; for as befitted a Son he was saying to the one who gave him birth without spot: Come, honored Lady, be glorified with your Son and God.

The choir of the Apostles shrouded your Body, which had received God, as they looked with awe and addressed you with clear voice: As you depart into heavenly bridal chambers to your Son, may you ever save your inheritance.

Second Canon.

Megalynarion, sung as the one above:
Angels, when they saw the falling Asleep of the Virgin, were amazed at how the Virgin went up from earth to the things on high.

Irmos.

Let all those born of earth, bearing torches, in spirit leap for joy; let the nature of the immaterial Minds keep festival as it honors the sacred festival of God's Mother, and let it cry out: Hail, all-blessed Mother of God, pure and ever-virgin'.

Troparia

Come now, on Zion, the divine and fertile mountain of the living God, let us be glad as we gaze on the Mother of God. For as his Mother Christ translates her to a far better and more divine tabernacle, the Holy of Holies.

Come, you faithful, let us approach the tomb of God's Mother, and let us embrace it, touching it sincerely with the lips, eyes and brows of the heart; and let us draw abundant gifts of healings, which flow from an ever-owing fount.

Receive from us this burial hymn, O Mother of the living God; and overshadow us with your light-bearing and divine grace. Grant victories to our Sovereign, peace to the people that loves Christ, to us who sing forgiveness and salvation of our souls.

Exapostilarion. Tone 3.

O you Apostles, assembled here from the ends of the earth, bury my body in Gethsemane; and you, my Son, receive my spirit. *(Three times)*
At Lauds insert 4 Stichera, doubling the 1st.

Tone 4.

At your glorious Falling Asleep the heavens rejoice and the armies of Angels exult; the whole earth is glad as it utters its funeral hymn to you, Mother of the Master of all things, all-holy Virgin, who knew not wedlock, who have delivered the human race from the ancestral sentence.

At a divine command the chief Apostles hastened from the ends of the earth to bury you, and when they saw you being taken from the earth to heaven they cried out with joy in Gabriel's words: Hail, chariot of the whole Godhead; hail, who alone by your childbirth have joined together things on earth with those on high.

Virgin Mother, Bride of God, who gave birth to life, you have passed over to immortal life by your revered Falling Asleep. Angels, Rulers and Powers, Apostles, Prophets and all creation escorted you, and your Son received in his immaculate hands your unblemished soul.

Glory to the Father and to the Son and to the Holy Spirit, now and ever and unto the ages of ages. Amen.

Tone 6.

At your immortal Falling Asleep, O Mother of God, Mother of life, clouds caught the Apostles up into the air; and though they were scattered through the world, made them form a single choir in the presence of your immaculate body. As they reverently buried you they sang Gabriel's song, crying out: 'Hail, full of grace, Virgin Mother without bridegroom, the Lord is with you'. With them implore him as your Son and our God that our souls may be saved.

Great Doxology.

BIBLIOGRAPHY

Ballew, Richard, managing ed. *The Orthodox Study Bible*. Nashville: Thomas Nelson, 2008.

Boss, Sarah Jane, ed. *Mary: the Complete Resource*. Oxford: Oxford University Press, 2007.

Daley, Brian. "'At the Hour of Our Death': Mary's Dormition and Christian Dying in Late Patristic and Early Byzantine Literature," *Dumbarton Oaks Papers*, Vol. 55 (2001), pp. 71-89.

_____, trans. *On the Dormition of Mary: Early Patristic Homilies*. Crestwood: St. Vladimir's Seminary Press, 1998.

Elliot, James Keith. *The Apocryphal New Testament*. Oxford: Clarendon Press, 1993.

Faculty of Holy Cross Greek Orthodox School of Theology, trans. *The Divine Liturgy of St. John Chrysostom*. Brookline: Holy Cross Orthodox Press, 1985.

Florovsky, Georges. *Creation and Redemption: Vol. 3 in the Collected Works of Georges Florovsky*. Belmont, MA: Nordland Publishing, 1976.

Gambero, Luigi. *Mary and the Fathers of the Church: The Blessed Virgin Mary in Patristic Thought.* San Francisco: Ignatius Press, 1999.

Hansbury, Mary, trans. Jacob of Serug. *On the Mother of God.* Crestwood: St. Vladimir's Seminary Press, 1998.

Holy Apostles Convent. *The Life of the Virgin Mary, the Theotokos.* Buena Vista, CO: Holy Apostles Convent, 1989.

Hopko, Thomas. *All the Fullness of God.* Crestwood: St. Vladimir's Seminary Press, 1982.

_____. *The Orthodox Faith*, Vol. 1 *Doctrine*, 2nd ed. Orthodox Church in America, Department of Religious Education, 1976.

Johnson, Elizabeth A. "The Symbolic Character of Theological Statements about Mary," *Journal of Ecumenical Studies*, 22:2, Spring 1985, 312-335.

Kelly, J. N. D. *Early Christian Doctrines.* Peabody: Prince Press, 2007.

Mastratonis, George. *A New-Style Catechism of the Eastern Orthodox Faith for Adults.* St. Louis: OLOGOS, 1977.

Maunder, Chris. "Mary in the New Testament and the Apocrypha." in *Mary, The Complete Resource.* Sarah Jane Boss, ed. Oxford: Oxford University Press, 2007.

Meyendorff, John. *Living Tradition*. Crestwood: St. Vladimir's Seminary Press, 1978.

Mother Mary and Ware, Archimandrite Kallistos, trans. *The Festal Menaion*. South Canaan, PA: St. Tikhon's Seminary Press, 1998.

Ouspensky, Leonid. *The Theology of the Icon*. Crestwood: St. Vladimir's Seminary Press, 1978.

Patrinacos, Nicon D. *A Dictionary of Greek Orthodoxy*. Pleasantville: Hellenic Heritage Publications, 1987.

Pelikan, Jaroslav. *Mary Through the Centuries: Her Place in History and Culture*. New Haven: Yale University Press, 1996.

Price, Richard. "Theotokos: The Title and its Significance in Doctrine and Devotion" in *Mary, The Complete Resource*. Sarah Jane Boss, ed. Oxford: Oxford University Press, 2007.

Schaff, Phillip and Roberts, Alexander, eds. *The Ante-Nicene Fathers*, Vol.1, Peabody, MA: Hendrickson, 1999.

Schmemann, Alexander. *The Eucharist*. Crestwood, NY: St. Vladimir's Seminary Press, 1988.

_____. *The Virgin Mary: Celebration of Faith, Vol. 3*. John A. Jillions, trans. Crestwood, NY: St. Vladimir's Seminary Press, 1995.

Shoemaker, Stephen. "Marian Liturgies and Devotion in Early Christianity," in *Mary, The Complete Resource*. Sarah Jane Boss, ed. Oxford: Oxford University Press, 2007.

_____. "Death and the Maiden: The Early History of the Dormition and Assumption Apocrypha," *St. Vladimir's Theological Quarterly* 50:1-2 (2006) 59-97.

Vassiliadis, Nikolaos P. *The Mystery of Death*. Peter A. Chamberas, trans. Athens, Greece: The Orthodox Brotherhood of Theologians "The Savior", 1993.

Ware, Timothy. *The Orthodox Church*. London: Penguin, 1987.

Wright, W., trans. "The Departure of My Lady Mary From This World", in *The Journal of the Sacred Literature and Biblical Record*. VII, 1965, pp. 129-160.

INTERNET RESCOURCES ON THE DORMITION

Anastasis.org. The hymnography of Fr. Ephrem Lash.

Ancient Faith Radio. Ancientfaith.com. Type "Dormition" in the search box to select from numerous interviews and reflections on the Falling Asleep of the Mother of God.

Antiochian Orthodox Archdiocese of North America. "Dormition of the Most Holy Theotokos." http://www.antiochian.org/node/20268.

Greek Orthodox Archdiocese of America. "Feast of the Dormition of our most Holy Lady, the Theotokos and Ever-Virgin Mary." http://goarch.org/special/listen_learn_share/dormition/index_html.

Monachos.net. "Services of the Dormition of the Theotokos." http://www.monachos.net/content/liturgics/liturgical-texts/677. Also at this site: "Lamentations of the Dormition of the Theotokos."http://www.monachos.net/content/liturgics/liturgical-texts/678.

Orthodox Church in America. "Dormition of the Theotokos." http://www.oca.org/OCchapter.asp?SID=2&ID=87.

The Orthodox Page. St. Gregory Palamas. "A Homily on the Dormition of Our Supremely Pure Lady Theotokos and Ever-Virgin Mary." http://www.ocf.org/OrthodoxPage/reading/dormition.html.

Orthodox Wiki. "Dormition." http://orthodoxwiki.org/Dormition.

NOTES

NOTES

NOTES